A Hundred [illegible]

CAOS

A nostalgic trip through the Society's archives

RAY TREAGUST

Very best wishes
Ray Treagust

MusicPrint

A Hundred Years of CAOS

ISBN 978-0-9565090-0-0

Published by:
MusicPrint
5 Lime Close
Chichester
West Sussex
PO19 6SW

A CIP catalogue record of this book can be obtained from the British Library.

Book set in Utopia 11/13.2
Designed by Michael Walsh
at MusicPrint, Chichester

and printed by
Ashford Colour Press
Unit 600 Fareham Reach
Fareham Road
Gosport
Hants PO13 0FW

Front cover image taken from the Society's publicity material for *The Mikado,* probably from the 1930s

CHAIRMAN'S MESSAGE

Affiliated to the
National Operatic and Dramatic Association

It is my pleasure to write a few words at the start of this exciting account of CAOS's history. As the present Chairman of the company I feel honoured indeed to be holding the reins as we move forward into the next century.

I believe we should be fiercely proud of our heritage and realise what a huge debt of gratitude we owe to those who founded our society one hundred years ago and to all the men and women who had the vision and drive to push it forward to make CAOS Musical Productions what it is today.

Over the years we are extremely fortunate to have had so many talented people in CAOS, and not only singers and actors. There are, of course, always sets to be designed and built and props and costumes to be collected or made; decisions to be made about the content of shows; musical direction, orchestras and directors to be found. There are the committee members who work so tirelessly on our behalf and the folk who make the tea at rehearsals. All these people deserve a vote of thanks, as without them where would the society be?

May I, on behalf of all members of the company, past and present, thank Ray Treagust, author of this wonderful book, for devoting his time in researching the content and to Michael Walsh for his part in setting it out so beautifully and publishing it for our enjoyment.

I am sure it will become a much loved and treasured possession for us all.

Elizabeth Peacock

LIST OF COLOUR PLATES

Most of the CAOS photographer's names have sadly disappeared in the mists of time, but in remembering them all we would like particularly to thank ***John Davidson****, who must have taken a great many of these,* ***Elizabeth Peacock****,* ***Rob Clark****, and most recently to* ***Ali Kittermaster*** *of Blush Photography (www.blushphotography.co.uk) for her photos of* Hello, Dolly!

blush
photography

FOREWORD

Chichester Amateur Operatic Society (affectionately known as CAOS) was formed as a Gilbert and Sullivan Society on the 6th May 1910 by the Cathedral Organist, Frederick Crowe, some of the Lay Vicars (the ancient name for the adult singers in the choir) and local businessmen. Early closing day in Chichester at that time was Thursday afternoon and both rehearsals and matineés were arranged for that day.

The Society is now a registered charity, but before attaining this status a great deal of the profits from various performances were donated to charities where it was considered appropriate.

Unfortunately, although we have minutes of early meetings of the Society, from 1912 onwards until 1927, we have very few details of events. We have however, a wonderful selection of photographs, and hope where details are not available, you will find pleasure in perusing through the pictures. To many we hope it will bring back happy memories.

Our hundred years would not have been possible without the work and dedication of many loyal members. May the Society continue to give pleasure to members and audience alike for many years to come.

Ray Treagust

1911

The first performance by the Society was **Pirates of Penzance** on the 18th and 19th January. You will probably be able to recognise from the poster shown opposite, the profession of some of the cast. For example :-

J & F. Hooper – Florists,

D. Howard – Butcher,

T.F. Lummus – Electrical,

H. Chaffer – Printer,

Rands – Hairdresser etc.

You will notice the performance was given at the Corn Exchange, which is now Next in East Street. When the theatre was filled and no further seats available, it was possible to sit on a corn bin. One dear lady advised that she had actually been seated this way for the price of 6d.

Proceeds from the show were donated to the local infirmary but we are unable to establish from our records how financially successful this was.

* * * * *

On page 4 is a photograph of the operetta taken by the company of Edgar Ward, Southsea. Why the body is lying on the stage in Pirates is rather odd. We believe it to be Ruth, on the other hand, has somebody shot the producer?

The Mikado was also performed in 1911 but unfortunately we have no details or photographs relating to this particular show.

CORN EXCHANGE,

CHICHESTER.

WEDNESDAY, JAN. 18th,

AT 8.15 P.M., and

THURSDAY, JAN. 19th, 1911

AT 3 P.M., and 8.15 P.M.,

THE CHICHESTER AMATEUR OPERATIC SOCIETY

(President—The Right Hon. the Countess of March)

Will present (by kind permission of Mrs. D'Oyly Carte), Gilbert & Sullivan's Original Comic Opera, "The

PIRATES OF PENZANCE,'

Or "THE SLAVE OF DUTY,"

In Aid of Chichester Infirmary.

CASTE.

Major General Stanley ... ... Mr. W. T. COLE.
The Pirate King ... ... Mr. REGINALD STEWART.
Samuel (His Lieutenant) ... ... Mr. JACK PETRIE.
Frederick (The Pirate Apprentice) ... ... Mr. ROBERT MARLEY.
Sergeant of Police ... ... Mr. ERN MILES.
Mabel (General Stanley's Daughters.) ... ... Miss CLARE LILLYWHITE.
Edith (General Stanley's Daughters.) ... ... Mrs. REGINALD STEWART.
Kate (General Stanley's Daughters.) ... ... Mrs. WILL. SINDEN.
Isabel (General Stanley's Daughters.) ... ... Miss DOROTHY KERWOOD.
Ruth (Pirate Maid of all Work) ... ... Miss KATRINE ST. CLAIR.

CHORUS of Pirates, Police, General Stanley's Daughters: Mesdames G. T. Apps, W. V. Cook, H. R. Cutten, R. W. Dawtrey, A. T. Humphry, W. H. Rands, R. F. Weller; Misses R. Charge, M. A. Dix, E. Hall, J. Hooper, F. Hooper, D. Howard, D. Kimbell, E. Lake, D. Lake, H. Napper, M. Purchase, E. Willis, N. Willis; Messrs. A. H. Caiger, L. Chaffer, H. Cresswell, C. W. Daughtry, H. H. Dyer, L. Evans, H. Furniss, C. Hall, W. Jones, E. H. Lake, T. F. Lummus, F. H. Manners, W. H. Rands, W. Whiteside, W. G. Willis.

FULL ORCHESTRA.

ACT I. .. .. A Rocky Seashore on the Coast of Cornwall.
ACT II. .. . . Ruined Chapel by Moonlight.

Hon. Conductor...MR. H. BRODIE. Hon. Stage Manager...MR. EDGAR WARD.
Hon. Secretary ... ... (23, South St., Chichester) MR. REG. B. STEWART.

Costumes, Wigs, Scenes and Effects, by Drury. Electric Lighting by Messrs. Strange & Son, Ltd., Chichester. Limelight Effects by Messrs. R. W. Dawtrey and G. Kemp.

Evening Performances: Doors open at 7.45; Early Door 7.30.
Matinee: Doors open at 2.30; Early Doors, 2.15.

Early Doors at all Performances 6d. extra to Unreserved Seats. Tickets purchased before dates of Performances admit to early doors without extra charge.

Prices of Admission: Matinee: Reserved Seats 5s. & 3s.; Unreserved Seats 2s.; Admission 1s.

Evenings: Reserved Seats, 4s. & 3s.; Unreserved 2s.; Admission 1s.

Carriages at 5 p.m. and 10.15 p.m.

Seats booked at Pillow & Sons, The Cross, Chichester, where Plans of the Hall may be seen

T. G. Willis & Co., Printers, 21, East Street, Chichester.

1912

Minutes of a committee meeting held on the 10th December 1912 at 52 East Street are the earliest records held. Mr. F. W. Crowe chaired the meeting but an odd entry in the minutes book shows Mr. W. T. Cole as the 'Hon. Sec. and Asstd Hon. Sec'. 2

Apparently, on the 15th January 1911, a social had been held and the committee agreed to pay a balance of 7s. 6 1/2 d. due from this event to the Hon Sec. (and presumably the Asstd. Hon. Sec.). Neither seemed particularly happy with the delay because they both resigned.

Iolanthe was the chosen operetta and as you can see from the photographs, the costumes for this show were quite magnificent. They show Miss Ada Gibbons in the named role of Iolanthe (1 below), Mr. R. Marley as Strephon (2), Miss Ethel Harman as Queen of the Fairies (3) and Mr. W. T. Cole as the Lord Chancellor (4). Another well-known business man, Mr. George Bevis, performed as Private Willis.

1

2

3   4

The sum of £20.8s.0d. was retained by the Society from Iolanthe, with £1.0s.0d. being donated to the Chichester Infirmary and a further £5.0s.0d. to the Orchestral Society.

It appears to have been quite a difficult period for the committee, as only thirteen days after the resignation of Mr. Cole, two further resignations were accepted. At the December meeting authorisation was given to the Treasurer to settle outstanding accounts from Iolanthe, with the exception of two pending an enquiry. It seems unfortunate that one account to be queried was submitted by a trader who happened to be a member of the Society. Being Christmas, would Scrooge have been more appropriate?

1913

Mr. G. W. Turnbull became chairman and one proposal submitted at an early meeting related to Society members from the Cathedral who were participating on stage. It reads:-

"The committee unanimously recommend that Lay Vicars, being active members of the Society, be reimbursed for any loss of bona fide engagements they might sustain during the performances and dress rehearsal of an opera."

It was decided that **HMS Pinafore** be selected as the operetta for 1913. Normal procedure at this time, was for a show to be named at the AGM for consideration and agreement by the members.

Some controversy appears to have resulted from a proposed increase in the price of the committee meeting room at 55 East Street. The committee's reply to the person requesting the increase reads "Terms could not be considered, the Society is willing to continue using the room on the same terms as they at present use it, viz 5/- per week, plus extras for fire and light, subject to a week's notice on either side."

HMS Pinafore was performed at the Corn Exchange in November. Although not known at the time, this was the last show for a period of five years owing to the interference of Kaiser Bill starting World War I. Some people have no thought for others.

An interesting item is transport provided to the society's performances. In the records it shows that on the 19th November, the Selsey tramway agreed to run a special late train for the society, with a cheap fare of 9d return for which a guarantee of 30/-, which was accepted.

HMS PINAFORE, 1913

Ethel Harman as Little Buttercup

H J Morgan – Boatswain's Mate,
W. Barcham as Dick Deadeye

Robert Marley as Ralph Rackstraw

Left: Reginald Stewart as Captain Corcoran with his wife as Josephine,
Right: Will T. Cole as Sir Joseph Porter,
Dorothy Kenwood as Hebe

At the AGM on the 6th February the audited accounts showed a balance of £19.18s.3d. and after "long discussion and criticism" the same be adopted. (Some things never change) £8.6s.1d. was allocated as follows:

Inmates of Dear's Almshouses	£2.10s.0d.
St. Johns Ambulance	£1.1s.0d.
Royal West Sussex Hospital	£4.15s.1d.

Patience was the chosen opera for the year but at a meeting arranged on the 7th September an entry reads:-

"The production is indefinitely postponed owing to the war."

(see copy overleaf)

September 7th/14

A. Committee Meeting was held @ St. Peters House, North Street, Chichester on Monday Sept 7th/14 @ 8.30 p.m.

Present Mr Crowe (Chairman) Messrs H. Lake, C. Hall, E. Miles, A.H. Caiger and the Hon. Sec.

The Minutes of the previous meeting held on Aug 7th were read & signed.

It was unanimously resolved that the Hon. Sec write a letter of condolence on behalf of the Society to Mrs Allrow on the sad loss sustained by her through the death of her husband, a genial & popular member of the Society.

It was also decided to send a wreath from the Society in the form of a Life Buoy with the words H.M.S. Pinafore worked in purple on a white ground.

Patience; The production was indefinitely postponed owing to the war.

This concluded the business of the Meeting:-

Fred J. W. Crowe.
Chairman

The last Committee Minutes before the Society was closed down during the years of the First World War.

1919

The first committee meeting after the war was held on the 28th February followed by a Special General Meeting on 7th March. The meeting was to discuss "The advisability of resuming rehearsals."

Apparently, "In spite of inclement weather, a good attendance of 20 members were present."

Pirates of Penzance was proposed but did not receive a seconder and it was duly decided to proceed with the missing performance of **Patience**.

Application was made at this time to join the National Operatic and Dramatic Association (NODA).

For the performances of **Patience**, the Corn Exchange requested 35% of gross takings, but the Society retaliated with an offer of 30%. Should the opera not be successful, ten members of the Society offered donations of £5 each.

Arrangements were made for special late trains to be laid for Selsey, Bognor and Emsworth district during the period of the show. (Obviously, some things do change).

Winnie Clemens, Evelyn Hall and Lilllian Ballard

Mrs AG Pink (Margo's mother) *Rose Robey as Lady Jane*

Will Cole as Bunthorne, Dragoon Officers Harry Simpson, George Bevis and Walter Lumley; opposite page : Freda Foster as Patience

Due to the number of people wanting to join the Society a motion was proposed by the committee to the effect :-

"all members should undergo a further trial before commencement of operatic rehearsals." Trial sounds rather drastic and perhaps audition would have been a more appropriate word. However, the trial consisted of :-

a. Vocal Test
b. Libretto
c. Stage Presence
d. Known Quantities

The above proposition was put to a Special General Meeting and carried by three votes.

Certainly, membership caused some concern as it was found necessary to make a further ruling:- "all new members should form a reserve to be drafted into the chorus when the necessity occurred." All names were then placed on a waiting list and admitted to active membership as suitable vacancies became available. Members on the waiting list could however audition for principal parts.

The Gondoliers was the chosen opera and you will see from the photographs that if you had a principal role, you were entitled to two beauty spots. Male or female, young or not so young, one spot on the cheek and one on the chin (or was there a measles epidemic?)

CAOS was to benefit from one fifteen year old young lady joining them in 1920, the first stage appearance of Miss Margaret Pink (Margo). The Society at that time could not ever anticipate the dedication and professionalism this young lady would bring to the company.

Margo Pink, aged 15

L to R: (back) Marco – Joseph Williams, Gianetta – Marguerite (Daisy) Horner, Giuseppe – Mark Hughes, Tessa – Winnie Clemens, Don Alhambra – George Bevis, Duchess – Hilda Wickham, Duke – Will Cole (seated) Casilda – Freda Foster, Luiz – Herbert Caiger.

L to R: Luiz – Herbert Caiger, Duchess – Hilda Wickham, Duke – Will Cole, Casilda – Freda Foster

Chorus of Gondoliers, 1920

Chorus of Contadini, 1920

1921

Yeomen of the Guard was selected as the operetta to be performed at the Corn Exchange, with the agreed cost being "£30 to £35 (in any case not to exceed £40) inclusive of all expenses, for one week."

One amusing entry in the October minutes :- "Headsmen – the Hon. Sec. was requested to approach Mr. W. Parker and failing him was to make the best arrangements possible." (Poison?)

The opera would appear to have been successful with donations made to Dears Almshouses to the value of £5.5s.0d. and a further £1.19s.4d. to the Actors' Benevolent Fund.

Left: William Parker as the Headsman.

Above: L to R: Frances Frost as Phoebe, Marguerite Horner as Elsie, Margaret Reede as Kate; kneeling lady unknown!

1922

The year commenced with a letter from the Corporation thanking the Society for the donation of £5.5s.0d. which had been "divided amongst the five old ladies in the Almshouses."

Originally, it was decided to perform Princess Ida, but after some discussion **The Sorcerer** and **Trial by Jury** were agreed upon. Unusually, The Sorcerer was staged before Trial.

Fees for the Corn Exchange were again raised as the owner stated he was unable to hold on to the previous agreement. He suggested the fee should be £40 and 25% of the net profits. This was considered excessive and it was proposed the Society should offer £40 and 20% of net profits. As seat prices ranged from 1/3 to 5/- the terms could appear high, but the terms suggested by the owner were eventually agreed upon.

There would appear to have been difficulty with people sneaking in without paying at the stage door and it was proposed :- "That a man be employed to keep the stage door and be paid 30/-, and also that each member entitled to use the door be supplied with a badge."

A unique form of advertising by postcards, as shown, was used for the first time.

Trial by Jury, 1922 : Dorothy Wentworth and Herbert Caiger

The Sorcerer 1922 : Will T. Cole as John Wellington Wells

Trial by Jury 1922: The Plaintiff and Bridesmaids

The Sorcerer, 1922

Left: Alexis – Walter Lumley, Aline – Marguerite Horner
Right: Mrs Partlett – Lilian Lowe, Constance – Susie Freeman

Above: Sir Marmaduke Pointdextre – John T. Jarman, Lady Sangazure – Hilda Wickham

Right: George Bevis as Dr. Daly

"By a ballot of members it was decided that The Pirates of Penzance be the opera for our next production," however, this was later changed to Mikado.

Once again terms were the subject most relevant. The Corn Exchange was now requesting a minimum of £75, with a sum of £45 to be paid on the first night.

Arrangements were made to meet the Directors of the Picturedrome, this being in Northgate (later the bus station.) The final offer from the Picturedrome was £85 for the week and 50% of the net profit. It was also proposed the Society would share the cost of erecting a stage. This arrangement, a three year agreement, was proposed and accepted by the society. There must have been great dissatisfaction with the Exchange.

In later minutes it shows the stage cost CAOS £83, shed (to store the stage?) £19.4s.0d., erection and dismantling £7.15s.0d. Later records show a further payment of £11.3s.0d. to make the shed waterproof.

All photographs of people who appeared onstage at that time were printed on postcards and sold in small booklets. Books of six photos were printed at 6/-, a book of 12 at 10/6. If you preferred postcard photos without the book – 7/6 per dozen.

Chichester Amateur Operatic Society.

THE PICTUREDROME,
CHICHESTER.

Nov. 20th to 24th, 1923

Tues., Wed., Thurs. & Fri. at 7.30.
Sat. at 8. Matinee Thurs. at 2.30.

THE MIKADO

(By permission of Mr. R. D'Oyly Carte).

Full Chorus & Orchestra 60 Performers.

Hon. Musical Director—Mr. F. J. W. Crowe.
Hon. Stage Manager—Mrs W. T. Cole.
Opera Produced by—Mr. Harry Drury, Sen.

Res. Seats, 5/- & 3/6 ; Unreserved, 2/4 ;
Admission, 1/3 (including Tax).

Seats Booked at Willis,' 21, East St., Chichester,
(Tel. 107) where Plans of the Hall may be seen.

Joint Hon. Secretaries—
Percy E. H. Lewis, Cawley Gate, Chichester,
H. E. Ball, 4, Oving Rd., Chichester. [Tel. 135.

STAFFORD & CO., LTD., PRINTERS, NETHERFIELD, NOTTS.

The reverse side of the advertising postcards in use at the time (see book cover for an example of the front).

THE MIKADO, 1923

1924

Three operas were put before a Special General Meeting, Pirates of Penzance, which received 13 votes, Iolanthe 27 votes and Ruddy Gore which received 17 votes. You will note the original name for Ruddigore shown in the minutes. Apparently, the original title was changed because The Graphic thought the title all right for men but it would 'scarcely sound pretty on ladies lips.'

An estimate for staging and dressing Iolanthe was £75. Dress rehearsals were always very strict on attendance – kept very private. 'It was decided that no one but members of the company, orchestra and those necessary for dressing be admitted to the dress rehearsal.' Cost of orchestra – 'That it be left to the Sub-Committee to do the best they could.'

The old 'chestnut' of people attending rehearsals appears in the minutes on a regular basis, with the committee being adamant that any person missing three rehearsals (later amended to four) without good reason should be dismissed from the cast. Hon. Accompanist for Iolanthe was Mrs. P. Lewis and Hon. Assistant Accompanist Miss M. Pink, who was also Iolanthe.

IOLANTHE, 1924

The Queen of the Fairies.

IOLANTHE, 1924

Above: Strephon and Phyllis

Right: Margo Pink as Iolanthe

1925

At the February meeting of all members it was suggested that the Society go outside Gilbert and Sullivan for the next production.

Originally postcards were sent to all members advising that Pirates of Penzance and Ruddigore had been proposed and if they were unable to attend the Special General Meeting arranged, to vote by proxy. Pirates won quite handsomely, but a further proposal was made and seconded, that a vote should be taken for Pirates and Les Cloches de Cornville. G and S won the day.

Chichester Amateur Operatic Society.

The PICTUREDROME, CHICHESTER.

November 24th to 28th, inclusive, 1925.

THE PIRATES OF PENZANCE

(By kind permission of Mr. R. D'Oyly Carte.)

Tuesday, Wednesday, Thursday and Friday at 7.30.

RESERVED SEATS 5/- & 3/6.

UNRESERVED SEATS 2/4.

ADMISSION 1/3. Including Tax.

Saturday at 8.

Matinee Thursday at 2.30.

SEATS BOOKED at the PICTUREDROME Tel. 208.

BOOKING HOURS :— 10 to 1, and 2 to 6.

Full Chorus and Orchestra of 75 Performers.

Hon. Musical Director—Mr. F. J. W. Crowe.

Hon. Stage Manager—Mrs. W. T. Cole.

Opera produced by Mr. Harry Drury, Senior.

Joint Hon. Secs. Percy E. H. Lewis, Cawley Gate, Chichester. Tel. 135; H. E. Ball, 4, Oving Road, Chichester.

It was decided week commencing 23rd November be the date for staging the opera, which happened to be a rather unfortunate choice. The question was raised regarding the abandonment of the Friday performance "on the occasion of the funeral of the late Queen Alexandra." However, it was thought that patrons who had booked for Friday and were living at a distance would be put to great hardship and it would be quite impossible to let them know what had taken place.

The Mayor suggested that if the net profits of the performance were devoted to charity he could see no objection to the performance being held. He agreed to see the Dean on this matter. Finally, put before an extraordinary meeting held at the Picturedrome, it was agreed that net profits from the whole show be given to charity.

PIRATES OF PENZANCE, 1925

PIRATES OF PENZANCE, 1925

1926

The committee were still negotiating with the Corn Exchange, who were asking for 50% of gross takings, which was considered "too heavy." CAOS made an offer of 35% on the first £200 and 25% on the remainder. After receiving a rejection of their offer, it was decided to obtain an estimate from the Picturedrome and both be considered. Eventually the Corn Exchange was accepted, terms – "£85 and 50% of the net profits." Ruddigore received more votes than four other operas submitted with their votes added together.

Mr. Drury retired as producer and a collection "not to exceed half a crown to purchase a suitable present as a recognition of his services to the Society" was made. This raised the sum of £4.15s.6d. Mrs. Cole, the new producer, Mrs. Lewis and the Chairman Mr. Crowe were allowed expenses to see Ruddigore at Brighton. Apparently, the opera had been continuously mentioned over previous years, but very little was known about it.

RUDDIGORE, 1926

Above left: Will Cole as Robin Oakapple

Above right:

Ernest Allnutt as Sir Despard Murgatroyd and Zena Cole as Mad Margaret

Right: Tommy Targett as Richard Dauntless

1927

The **Gondoliers** was again the chosen opera. Owing to the strength of the ladies' chorus it was resolved that "all new ladies elected on 25th February should be advised that they could only become Active Members of the society as vacancies occurred."

£50 was donated to the Royal West Sussex Hospital from the reserve fund of the Society and it was proposed that a further minimum sum of £50 be forwarded from the future production of Gondoliers.

An entry in our records relates to the late Mr. F. Longlands:- "It was specially desired that sympathetic reference be recorded in these minutes of the lamented death of our late friend and member, who would always be remembered with esteem and affection." It was also requested that photographs of the Society wreath were suitable placed in the minute book. We show one of the photographs on page 34 which remain in the minute book to this day.

£100 was forwarded to the Royal West Sussex Hospital Centenary Fund from the Gondoliers production. The Corn Exchange, now under new management and known as the Exchange Theatre, were suitably impressed by the opera and added a further 20 guineas to the Royal West Sussex Hospital fund. (see opposite page).

Two pages from the original programme are shown on pages 32-3. The advertisements around the programme will bring back many memories to Cicestrians of riper years!

Telephones.
CHICHESTER ~~184.~~ 407
GERRARD 3812.

Telegrams.
EXIMWAINRI,
PICCY, LONDON.

THE EXCHANGE THEATRE
CHICHESTER.
THE EXCHANGE THEATRE LTD.

DIRECTORS.
J. G. WAINWRIGHT.
D. M. WAINWRIGHT.
R. B. WAINWRIGHT.
R. W. LIMBERT.

REGISTERED OFFICES.
6/7 PICCADILLY MANSIONS,
SHAFTESBURY AVENUE, W. 1.
LONDON.

RBW/MH

7th December, 1927.

The Secretary,
Amateur Operatic Society,
CHICHESTER.

Dear Sir,

We beg to offer you our heartiest congratulations on the extraordinarily good performance your Society gave throughout last week in our Theatre.

We had a number of our personal friends present at the first night, which is not usually the best evening of the week, but they were all most impressed with the workmanlike and efficient way in which the whole of the Opera was carried through.

They thoroughly enjoyed the entertainment, and felt that for an Amateur Show, it was one of the best they had ever seen.

The writer joins with them in this opinion, and we feel most gratified that the strenuous efforts made by your Society have resulted in a good return from the public in entrance fees which will go to such a worthy cause as the West Sussex Hospital Centenary Fund.

We have pleasure in enclosing herewith on behalf of our company, a subscription to this fund of twenty guineas, which we trust will help to swell the total results of your worthy efforts.

Yours very truly,

ENCLOSURE:

R B Wainwright

UNDER ENTIRELY NEW MANAGEMENT.
No order or contract is valid unless signed by a Director of the Company.

THE CHICHESTER AMATEUR OPERATIC SOCIETY cordially invite applications for Membership from all musical Ladies and Gentlemen who are interested in Gilbert and Sullivan's Operas.

OPERAS PRODUCED.

"**The Pirates of Penzance**"	1911
"**The Mikado**"	1911
"**Iolanthe**"	1912
"**H.M.S. Pinafore**"	1913
"**Patience**"	1919
"**The Gondoliers**"	1920
"**The Yeoman of the Guard**"	1921
"**The Sorcerer**" and "**Trial by Jury**"	1922
"**The Mikado**"	1923
"**Iolanthe**"	1924
"**The Pirates of Penzance**"	1925
"**Ruddigore**"	1926
"**The Gondoliers**"	1927

This Society is Entered for the National Competition in Operatic Art.

PROGRAMME

The Gondoliers

Or "The King of Barataria."

[*In Aid of the Royal West Sussex Hospital Centenary Appeal Fund.*]

(By permission of Mr. R. D'OYLY CARTE).

Written by W. S. GILBERT. Composed by ARTHUR SULLIVAN.

Producer and Stage Manager, MRS. W. T. COLE.

ACT 1—Scene :
The Piazzetta, Venice.

ACT 2—Scene :
Pavilion in the Palace of Barataria.

(An interval of three months is supposed to have elapsed between Acts 1 & 2).

Costumes, Scenery, etc., by B. and H. DRURY, Brighton.

Light Refreshment may be obtained in the new Corn Exchange behind this Theatre during the Interval. Caterer : A. J. Wickham.

Floral tribute from CAOS at the funeral of Mr. F. Longlands.

THE GONDOLIERS

1927

Marco, Gianetta (Zena Cole), Tessa and Giuseppe.

Duchess of Plaza Toro, Casilda (Margaret Pink) and Luiz.

1928

Recorded in the Society records is a letter from the Duke of Richmond "Thanking the Society for their expression of sympathy in the loss of the late Duke, our President." Assets of the Society were published and make interesting reading :-

War Savings certificates original cost £ 284.8s.6d.,

now worth	£367.0s.0d.
Piano	£30.0s.0d.
Half share of stage at the Picturedrome	£10.0s.0d.
Stage cloth	10s.0d.
	£407.10s.0d.

HMS Pinafore and **Trial by Jury** were staged and estimates received to dress both amounted to "65 guineas, with 8 guineas extra if a change of costume was required in Pinafore." Master Marcus Longlands was selected for the part of Tom Tucker. Profit from the performances amounted to £56 from which a further donation of £50 was forwarded to the Royal West Sussex Centenary Fund.

It is most unfortunate that no records can be found between 1928 and 1952, although we have been very lucky to have a great number of photographs and a small number of newspaper cuttings. During 1939 to 1947 no operettas were actually performed owing to the Second World War.

Right: Little Buttercup

Ralph: Bernard Lewis, Josephine: Margo Pink, Sir Joseph: Will Cole.

Captain Corcoran (Ernest Allnutt) with Dick Deadeye

1930

Dorothy

*A selection of photographs from **Dorothy**; including Tommy Targett above right*

Opposite page: a wonderful panoramic shot of the Corn Exchange stage, including some members of the orchestra … and a pack of hounds !

1932

Yeomen of the Guard

1934

Ruddigore

The photographs show Mr George Bevis as Murgatroyd, Zena Cole as Margaret and Richard Dauntless who we believe was played by Bernard Lewis.

Phyllis Pointing who joined the Society from Halifax in 1933, is shown in her first principal role in the society as Rose Maybud.

Left: George Bevis Snr as Murgatroyd and Zean Cole as Mad Margaret

Phyl Pointing in her first principal role with CAOS

1936

Jolly Roger

In a copy of the programme kindly loaned by Ken Green, was found this note from Len Eyles:

Although the society had staged "Dorothy" in 1930 and "Merrie England" in 1931, the decision to attempt "Jolly Roger" was a really drastic break with the old G & S tradition. In fact there were considerable fears that some of the rather bawdy aspects of this very modern show might prove unacceptable to a Chichester audience and especially some of the society's august supporters like the Bishop (George Bell) and the Dean (Duncan-Jones). A very little watering-down may have been done, but the Bishop certainly expressed his delight at the end result and was not upset by a few "bloodies".

"The Officials" (almost the last page [of the programme]) make interesting reading and show what an extraordinary mixture of people were involved in the society. M T Hughes (Chairman) was the county treasurer. His committee included Les Hooker (son of the Hornet builder, Chas Hooker), Tommy Felton (a droll Lancastrian who was in some form of Govt. or local Govt. office), Len Chaffer the printer, Tommy Targett (an administrator at Graylingwell Mental Hospital) and my milkman father. The musical director, Arthur Trew, was the music expert at Charterhouse. This brings me to the Lewis family who, with the Cole family from Bognor, were the backbone of the society for many years. Percy and his wife Olive, with their son Bernard (Jolly Roger himself) lived just by the pedestrian railway crossing half-way between Stirling Road and the station. Percy and his brother (violinists both) were opticians in East Street. I don't recall what Bernard did, but he was an extremely talented youth who spoke several languages.

The orchestra included some very talented players such as Mrs Harvey Grace (wife of the cathedral organist and choirmaster) and the two Buckle ladies. Note also Gordon Stables (flute) who was physics master at the High School and F.J. Elderton (clarinet) who was a plumber living in Lyndhurst Road.

The list of vice-presidents is a real reflection of the local "establishment" in those days, although I can't for the life of me think where Princess Marie d'Orleans held her court. J.W. Loader-Cooper, as you are probably aware, was the very Pooh-Bah of Chichester – at one time Town Clerk, Clerk to the Justices, City Coroner, County Coroner, Coroner of the Hundred of Bosham and so on!

I don't know why I didn't get my name in this programme along with my father and his half-sister. I had a walk-on part as a soldier and had the pleasure of grabbing my father [Eric] by the scruff of the neck and bundling him off the stage every night of the week!

Ernest Allnutt and Tommy Felton

Two extracts from this special 25th year souvenir programme (by Willis of North Street) are worthy of quoting:

A BOLD EXCURSION

Perhaps the most onerous task, and one which imposes great responsibilities upon the Committee, is the choice of a work for production.

Our Society was not constituted to act as mere providers of! "popular entertainment," but as a body of workers seeking the improvement and propagation of the Art of Opera as a social exercise. It is therefore our duty to produce only those works which possess artistic merit and which will repay study, not at the Box-Office alone but which provide some educational advancement.

After many years study of the famous Savoy series of operas,' we decided to set to work upon more modern compositions and venturing, this year, into the realm of sheer burlesque we are fully conscious of making a bold excursion. To attempt to capture the spirit of burlesque is, for amateurs, a very hazardous adventure. We rely upon our long experience as a Society, and upon the stagecraft thereby acquired to assist us in pursuit of this elusive "sprite."

The burden cast upon the Society is a particularly heavy one inasmuch as there is no "traditional" or "professional" method of producing this work. We are urged by Mr. V. C. Clinton Baddeley (the author of the lyrics and part-author of the book) to avoid imitation of any previous production of the opera. This precept is being carefully observed, and the presentation now put before our audiences has been virtually "created" by ourselves. Mr. Clinton-Baddeley's injunction that "we produce the work as we ourselves read it" has been obeyed.

Both the scenery and the costumes have been specially made for this production—the first in Sussex—by Messrs. Drury, of Brighton, and no effort has been spared to ensure a happy evening for our guests.

OUR COMING-OF-AGE

The Chichester Amateur Operatic Society was born 25 years ago of the enthusiasm of a group of Cicestrians interested in amateur operatic work, many of whom have retained their interest right down to the present production—our coming-of-age production. A strict Savoy tradition was followed for several years, the ice being broken by "The Pirates of Penzance" which was followed by the "Mikado" in the same year, 1911. We were only four years old when the Great War cut several years out of our existence. Eight years after we were born (as a society) we were still only four years old, and the first of the post-war productions was appropriately "Patience," which was one of the finest shows we have ever put on. The tradition was maintained up to the present year, with the exceptions of "Dorothy" and "Merrie England."

The old society founded in 1910 included our present veterans, Will Cole and Mrs. Cole, Percy Lewis and Mrs. Lewis, and Len Chaffer, and in the company were some of the Cathedral lay vicars, and Mr. F. J. W. Crowe, who was the original musical director. Charles, Duke of Richmond and Gordon, was our first patron, and his family has always been keenly interested in our society. They have been our patrons ever since. We have also been fortunate in having the keen interest of the Earl and Countess of Bessborough, our presidents.

In our existence of a quarter of a century we have contributed several hundred pounds to local charities, but in the last few years of shortness of money, mechanised music, and increasing expenses, we have found it increasingly difficult to keep our heads above water. So many of the Chichester organisations have gone under through lack of support—the Chichester Musical Society and the Chichester Oratorio Society are but two instances. We may yet have to call on our vice-presidents.

1937

Princess Ida

Margot Pink

Phyllis Pointing

Audrey Bryant and Reg Bevis

Margaret Desarzens with ...?

1947

Thirty-seventh year of CAOS, but owing to two world wars, only their 25th production.

Owing to the fact that the Exchange Theatre was no longer available for its productions, the Society "has to content itself with the concert version of a Light Opera – for the first time in its history."

Merrie England (concert version) was held at the Assembly Room.

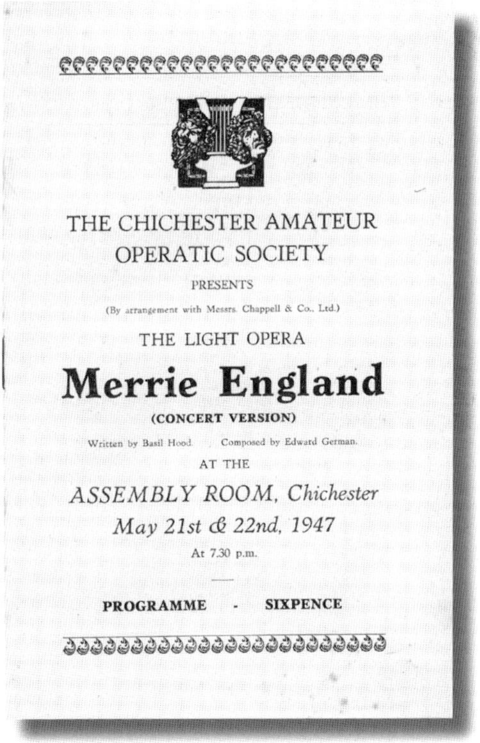
THE CHICHESTER AMATEUR OPERATIC SOCIETY
PRESENTS
(By arrangement with Messrs. Chappell & Co., Ltd.)
THE LIGHT OPERA
Merrie England
(CONCERT VERSION)
Written by Basil Hood. Composed by Edward German.
AT THE
ASSEMBLY ROOM, Chichester
May 21st & 22nd, 1947
At 7.30 p.m.
PROGRAMME - SIXPENCE

Three people performed who took part in the Society's first ever production:- Will T. Cole and Mr & Mrs. Percy Lewis. Hon. Conductor was cathedral organist Mr. H. A. Hawkins.

1948

Jolly Roger was performed as a concert version at the Assembly Room. Mutiny – when rehearsals started, the ladies took a poor view at first of the men's chorus singing about 'barratry, arson, rape and slaughter' and 'bloody pirate.' The report on the Hampshire Telegraph reads:- 'Mr Lewis said 'The Mutiny' has been squashed. The concert version will be adapted and I am writing to Clinton Baddeleley, who wrote the lyrics for his advice.'

1949

HMS Pinafore – the first live performance on stage since 1938.

Mentioned in the programme:- 'This year a full stage performance is once again being embarked upon, but under a severe handicap. The stage upon which HMS Pinafore is being produced is much too small for the players to do themselves real justice, and the inadequacy of the seating capacity of the hall [Assembly Room] makes this venture hazardous from the financial point of view. Had it not been for the extreme generosity of our Vice Presidents and others, this production would not have been in any way possible.'

'It is with regret the Society has to stress the deplorable fact that there is in Chichester today no theatre or stage available worthy of a Gilbert and Sullivan production.' What's new?

Every seat was sold and a loss made on the production accounts.

1949 HMS Pinafore ~ Midshipmate Deborah Goodger (Margo Pink's daughter)

1949 HMS Pinafore ~

Reg Bevis as Dick Deadeye

1949 HMS Pinafore ~

The Ladies' chorus

1950

"Operatic Society's hazardous adventure". These were the newspaper headlines relating to the earlier production of **HMS Pinafore**. At the AGM it was stated the cost of staging the show was £300 and it was only the willingness of the members to offset the estimated deficit of £300 that decided the society to go forward with the production. They contributed £44.17s.0d. in addition to their normal subscriptions but, the actual loss proved to be only £10.1s.1d.

During July, Chichester received a visit from the Chief of the Swedish Broadcasting Corporation, Nils Olof Franzen. For the latter part of his day, Mr Franzen was busy making records for inclusion in his broadcasts on the English way of life. His evening started with the Salvation Army band and later included "a miniature promenade concert" at the Assembly Room. The programme opened with a chorus and 73 year old Mr Arthur Pink sang "Sussex by the Sea" taking the solo as robustly as ever he did 40 years ago."CAOS sang extracts from The Mikado.

The show chosen for the year was **The Mikado**, shown in the press as a "masterly presentation, but too many encores. I stopped counting when the number reached 10." Profits: 6s. 2d.

1950 The Mikado ~ 'Three Little Maids' l to r: Pitti Sing ~ Jean Bevis, Yum Yum ~ Joan Felton, Peep Bo ~ Phyllis Shepherd

1951

A number of performances of "The Four Men" from the book by Hilaire Belloc, adapted by the Lord Duncannon, were given in towns and villages in Sussex. The men of CAOS sang some of the choruses, travelling as far East as Lewes, where a combined performance was given with the Lewes Operatic Society.

CAOS members also performed at the Pier Pavilion, Worthing, with the Worthing Municipal Orchestra during February.

A report on the concert in the evening news read: "CAOS enjoying a sound reputation in their own city, but what is said about them outside? Their warm reception at Worthing municipal Pier Pavilion last evening is an encouraging indication. After their programme of solos, quartets and choruses, Coleman J, a former Worthing mayor, referred to them as "this very remarkable society." Chichester, he added, had long been famous for its cathedral – in future it should be well known for its operatic society."

1951 The Gondoliers ~ Top: Joan Felton as Gianetta; below: 'A regular Royal Queen' with E. Wood, J. Bevis, W. Kinshott & J. Felton

Following the society's performance of **the Gondoliers**, Margot was presented with a silver mounted baton. The baton is now held as a token of office by the current chairman.

1952

Probably the most ambitious performance of light opera was performed in Priory Park during June 1952, when Edward German's **Merrie England** was staged. Professional stars joined with CAOS and other amateurs under producer Thomas Bell and musical director Margaret Pink. These were cast as follows: Earl of Essex – Leslie Rands, Sir Walter Raleigh – Webster Booth, Gill-all-alone – Marjorie Eyre and Bessie Throckmorton – Anne Ziegler.

It was estimated that the opera would cost £2,000 to stage with profits to be given to the Eventide Housing Association. Apparently, costs had been covered by the Thursday performance and Eventide benefited by £500. Bookings for the opera amounted to over £8,000.

1952 Merrie England ~ Webster Booth and Anne Ziegler

1952 Merrie England ~ 'Come follow the drum'

1952 Merrie England ~ Tommy Felton, Andrew Bryant, C. Nisbet, S. Wellington

Can you imagine, a whole week, an open-air opera and no rain! Mr Dick Doman presented on behalf of the Eventide Homes, a silver cigarette case to Margot and a music case to "Dinger" Bell.

Webster Booth listed the qualifications of a concert singer when he attended the Rotary Club "Merrie England" lunch. "One must be an athlete, a student, a musician, a clerk, an accountant, a lawyer, a psychologist, a dress designer and a mannequin, or if a man a tailor's dummy," he said. "He had to be able to read at sight all kinds of music, play the piano a little, used a typewriter, understand railway timetables, grapple with managers and newspaper reporters, spot the awkward clauses in any contracts and be a real expert on income tax. He should also have a voice."

1953

An interesting article in the *Hampshire Telegraph and Post* states: "Balancing the account of an operatic production in the Assembly Room resembles a tightrope act – two years ago with full houses for every performance a profit of seven shillings and 8p was recorded. This (**Patience**) is the first major production in the renovated and re-equipped Assembly Room with hiring fees going up but no increase of seating accommodation.

In the hope of restoring the balance, 6d has been added to the price of the most expensive seats." The actual loss on the nine performances of Patience was £48. *(see Photos on p 56)*

1955

From the Chichester Observer:

Cicentrians can be grateful to the city's amateur operatic society for its presentation this week of another Gilbert and Sullivan opera – this time the popular **Ruddigore**.

1953 ~ Patience

1953 Patience   Grosvenor ~ Graham Stote-Blandy

Always delightful, the enchanting melodies and clever lyrics win full effect in the local performance of which Miss M. Pink is producer and musical director.

But what a shame that fuller scope for the opera is impossible in the Assembly Room's small stage!

There were one or two occasions on Friday night when congestion on stage threatened to turn the humorous show into something ludicrous.

An unwieldy chorus of professional bridesmaids and village maidens became a jostling crowd when partnered by the officers in a lively dance.

Ample compensation, however, was provided in the quality of the choruses and in the capable handling of major roles. None of the typically Gilbertian 'situations' was lost on the near-capacity audience."

1956

Quite a shock for officials of CAOS when they received a rate demand for £235 in respect of a large coloured notice which occupied the whole of an empty shop window next to the Assembly Room, advertising their **Yeomen of the Guard** production.

Apparently, a hurried interview with the city treasurer, Mr D A Palmer, was followed by an undertaking that the demand would be withdrawn to save administrative work if the Bill was removed. The notice, which had been made by members, was in fact on the outside of the window for a full week, which together with articles in the press made for excellent advertising.

Stage manager Mr JM Gilbert took the view that the local voluntary societies were a valuable asset to the city: "they are just as important as the North Walls, the Cathedral, the City Cross or Guildhall and the authorities should try to encourage them, not discourage them by acts such as this."

Yeomen was a great success with the following comment in *Sunlit*, the NODA magazine: "to all musical directors in the section, I say – do go and see the Chichester society if you can – the visit will be well worth while."

1958

Press reported: "vivacity and gaiety in comic opera. **The Gondoliers** makes brilliant entertainment."

1956 ~ Yeomen of the Guard Leonard Meryl ~ Philip Walter; Phoebe ~ Jeanne Bevis; Sergeant Meryl ~ Bernard Vick

1956 : Yeomen of the Guard

Doreen Harman as Elsie Maynard and Keith Parker as Colonel Fairfax

1958 - The Gondoliers ~ 'From the Sunny Spanish shore'

1960

The Observer, Friday May 13th: "Two world wars and the ravages of wartime entertainment have failed to bring to an end amateur opera in Chichester, and today, amid the applause of a faithful City audience, the local Society celebrates its golden jubilee."

The report mentions that a yellowing but well-prepared minute book (still held) records that the inaugural meeting took place at St Bartholomew's parish hall, Orchard Street, on Friday May 6th at 8.15. On May 13th, ladies and gentlemen numbering 40-45 cut a birthday cake in their Eastgate Hall rehearsal room.

Many interesting items are mentioned in the press report, some are as follows:

"those were the days when the stage was in the Corn Exchange (now Next) and a much more commodious stage it was than of the Assembly Room. The Society played there until 1938."

1984 : HMS Pinafore

above: Ray Treagust, Alison Mobbs and David Russell in full flight

below : at the real HMS Victory
l to r: Betty Treagust, Anthony Nixon, Jill Brazier, John Mason, Judith Russell and Bernard Vick

1986 : The Merry Widow at the Assembly Room

above: Les Grisettes; below: 'Women, women, women'

1994 : The cast of Die Fledermaus with CAOS President David Evershed-Martin centre

1995: Kismet ~ Christopher Doman, Vivienne Aitken, David Russell, Kym Willcocks and Simon Long

1996 : The Gondoliers ~ 'Bridegroom and Bride' being encouraged by MD Michael Walsh

1998 : Waltzes from Vienna ~ Christopher Doman as Johann Strauss and Robert Clark as Drexler

1998 : My Fair Lady ~ Nicola Russell as Eliza Doolittle

2000 : the cast of Oklahoma!

above: 2006 :
The Boyfriend

Christine Henry as Madame Dubonnet and Malcolm Graves as Percival Browne

right : 2007 :
Brigadoon

Kerrie Wenham as Fiona MacKeith and Andy Murray as Tommy Albright

2009: Guys and Dolls

Above: Michelle Walby and the Hot Box Girls

Right: Hélène Davies as Miss Adelaide

2010 : Hello, Dolly!

Right: Margo Dodd
as Mrs Irene Molloy and
Trevor Thurgood as
Cornelius Hackl

Below left: Kevin Casssidy
as Horace Vandergelder and
Amanda Crehan as
Dolly Gallagher-Levi

Below Right:
Claire Blake as Ermengarde

"Margaret Pink, whose father played the bones in a Minstrel troop running at the time of the formation, took over [as Musical Director] from Mr Hawkins in 1948."

"It is interesting that Mr Bevis is playing in this year's Mikado, the part, Pooh-Bah, which his father played in 1923."

Two operettas were performed to celebrate the 50 years, **The Pirates of Penzance** during May and **The Mikado** during October.

1969

Princess Ida : This production was a milestone in the musical career of Margot Pink. This was her 50th year with the society. As well as being producer and musical director, she was leading lady for nine productions, accompanist and played in the orchestra. Fate provided her 50th year with a memorable hurdle. Five weeks before the show the leading man, tenor Douglas Moore, had to cry off on doctor's orders.

1960 ~ Cutting the cake to celebrate 50 years of CAOS

Jeanne Bevis, ... Davis, Phyl Pointing, Jean Lee, June Wellington, Joyce Foote, June Coleman

Right: 1962 : The Sorcerer

Margaret Smart as Mrs Partlett

Below: 1962 : The Sorcerer

Judy Clifford as Lady Sangazure

John Mason as John Wellington Wells

Rather than import from another Society, the part of Prince Hilarion was given to Michael Swain, who was apparently not experienced in playing lead roles. Praise indeed in the press: "his voice is not much to speak of, but he played the part in an easy unruffled way, full of character and dash."

The 1969 / 1970 annual report records with great regret "the death of Guy A Reynolds which occurred in November. He was a staunch member of the society in its early years."

1969 : Princess Ida ~
Kevin Sivyer as Arac, Len Marchant as Guron and Jim Fielder as Synthius

1969 : Princess Ida ~ Paddy Dornom as Ida and Michael Swain as Hilarion

Below: 1971 : The Municipal Asset ~ Timothy Bastow as the night watchman

1971

Pirates of Penzance marked the diamond jubilee of CAOS. Pirates was preceded by **The Municipal Asset or the Penalty of Joining the Common Market**. A nicely satirical libretto was written by Keith Parker, a leading tenor of the society, ably set to music from the G and S operas by Margaret Pink.

Timothy Bastow played the part of the night watchman employed to guard the historic and antiquarian hole in the road – the municipal asset. Margaret Smart became the Mayor Elect and Douglas Moore the Common Market Negotiator.

1974 : Yeomen of the Guard

1974 : Yeomen of the Guard

Above : the full company

Left: Don Absolon as Leonard Meryll

Nancy Mathews as Phoebe

John Mason as Sgt Meryll

1975

The Society lost its most valuable member during the year with the death of Margaret Pink. It was felt the best tribute CAOS could pay to their late musical director and producer was to put on "a thundering good production of **HMS Pinafore**."

Joyce Foote stepped in to take over musical responsibility and Jean Beavis was the producer. **Pinafore** was a great success and a wonderful achievement for those who took over the reins.

1975: HMS Pinafore ~
Ann Bray as Little Buttercup and John Mason as Captain Corcoran

1975: HMS Pinafore

Right:

Keith Parker as Ralph Rackstraw

Paddy Dornom as Josephine

Below:

Ray & Betty Treagust as Sir Joseph Porter and Hebe

1977

To celebrate the Queen's Silver Jubilee, the society performed a concert version of **Merrie England** at the Assembly Room. Jean Bevis produced the concert, Sid Sivyer was musical director.

Members of CAOS also took part in a Gilbert and Sullivan "Sing in" at the Guildhall, Portsmouth during September.

During October, **The Mikado** was staged with the writeup in the Observer stating as follows: "Chichester Operatic amateur actors automatically start at a disadvantage, playing in the shadow of the city's Festival Theatre." The rest of the writeup, however, seems to think we are pretty good for amateurs. It hasn't been mentioned since.

1977 : Merrie England ~ soloists from this concert performance. The tall figure in the back row is Sid Sivyer, Musical Director

1977: The Mikado

Judith Lee as Peep-Bo

Paddy Dornom as Yum-Yum

Madeline Grant as Pitti-Sing

Below:

The full Company

1978 : The Gondoliers

Above: Christopher Williams as Giuseppe, Ann Hudson as Tessa, Madeleine Grant as Gianetta and Peter Cam as Marco

Right: Alfred Price as Don Alhambra and Kathleen Blake as Inez

Opposite page : 1979 : Ali Baba

from left: Ray Treagust, John Mason, John Davison, Jeff Stanbridge, Ron Williams, David Russell and Don Norton all hovering above Geoff Miller

1979

Quite a change for the society when they staged their first pantomime, **Ali Baba** during February. Leading role of Ali Baba was taken by Jim Fielder who was ably supported by such characters as Musthavit, Cudhavit, Stitchit and a rather delightful Camel, who incidentally appeared in suspenders on the last performance. Press headlines "lovely, lively, lots of laughs in this slick show."

1979 : Ali Baba ~ what a bevy of beauties!

Ruddigore followed in October. Tickets for CAOS shows at this time were obtainable from the Army and Navy store (Morants) in West Street. *(see photos opposite)*

1980

Following the success of the first pantomime it was decided to stage **Jack and the Beanstalk** during February. Hit of the show were the "Smurfs", a band of "cuddly creatures with baggy pants and blue noses", or that's how the press described them. It goes on to report "plenty of laughs came from their activities – they even upstaged Daisy the Cow, whose front and rear halves also doubled as "Smurfs" – they couldn't find any others to take the parts." *(see photos on page 74)*

1979 : Ruddigore

Ann Bray as Mad Margaret

Below:

the full cast

1980 : Jack and the Beanstalk ~ left: Pam Budd as Polly and Vivienne Aitken as Jack; right: Jim Fielder as Widow Twankey; below: "The Smurfs"

1980

1980 was the 70th anniversary of CAOS and in October they performed **Pirates of Penzance**. Trouble galore followed this particular show when a write-up by Jock Wilson appeared in the Observer running down not only the society but each and every performer. Mr. Wilson took a greater share of criticism the following week from the great number of letters published in support of a very fine show and a very poor critic.

1981

Aladdin was presented at the Assembly Room during February and the profit from the pantomime, £217, was presented to the Lions Club for their International Blood Research Appeal.

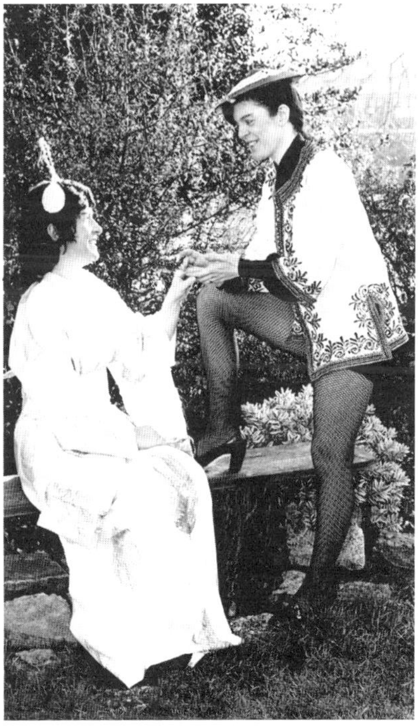

1981 : Aladdin ~ left: Geoff Miller, David Russell, Judith Russell and Betty Treagust, right: Pamela Budd and Vivienne Aitken

The 1981 GAla Day Float with CAOS's trophy.

On the event of Chichester Gala Day, CAOS entered a float of **Princess Ida** and won the Champions' Cup plus their class in the parade.

The parade also served to advertise the operetta which was performed during October. With a cast of 46, the Assembly Room stage again became a problem, cramping the cast for room and restricting the dancing scenes. According to press reports, however, it was clearly a success.

CAOS's year ended with a Concert of Christmas music held at St Paul's Church under the direction of Michael Walsh, organist Kevin Stannard and orchestral leader Edward Richards.

1982

Another change of programme to give variety, this time an **Old Tyme Music Hall**. This particular show gave a great number of people the opportunity to perform either a solo item or with a group, when normally they might miss out when auditioning for an operetta. On the last two performances, the audience were asked to dress up in the appropriate costume for the period and this proved to be a great success. **Iolanthe** was the chosen opera for October, the last show produced by Jean Bevis, who joined CAOS in

1936. Members paid tribute to Jean and her husband George, expressing gratitude for their wonderful contribution to the society and wishing them many happy years of retirement.

1982 : Old Tyme Music Hall ~ 'Direct from the Tower'

1982 : Iolanthe ~ with Margaret Schofield as Queen of the Fairies

Olde Tyme Music Hall

Presented by

Chichester Amateur Operatic Society

Written and Produced by Mr. Raymond Treagust.
Music Orchestrated and Directed by Mr. Michael Walsh.

24 - 27th March 1982

PROGRAMME

1	Strolling in the Park	—	Ladies and Gentlemen of the Chorus
2	John Peel	—	Mr. John Mason, Mr. Geoffrey Miller, Mr. David Russell, Mr. Raymond Treagust
3	Mrs. Ann Moss, Miss Judith Lee	—	Life's Dream is O'er
4	Uncle Tom Cobleigh	—	Gentlemen of the Chorus
5	A New Dress	—	Sketch regarding attire
6	The Drawing Room A Musical Extravaganza At the Piano - Mr David Russell		Mrs Paddy Dornom, Mrs Margaret Schofield Mr Anthony Nixon Mrs Betty Treagust, Mr Peter Cam Mr John Mason
7	Mr. Raymond Treagust	—	With the End of his Old Cigar
8	Mr. David Russell	—	Sunshine of Your Smile
9	Music of the War	—	Ladies and Gentlemen of the Chorus

INTERVAL of 15 minutes

Sweetmeats in the Foyer. Alcoholic Beverages, Soft Drinks and Coffee Downstairs

10	Our London	—	Ladies and Gentlemen of the Chorus
11	Have a Nice Time	—	Domestic Sketch
12	Direct from the Tower	—	Mrs. Margaret Schofield, Mrs. Betty Treagust, Mr. James Fielder
13	Mrs. Paddy Dornom, Mr. Anthony Nixon	—	The Golden Song — Lilac Time
14	Strength and Beauty	—	Study in Pose and Health
15	Mrs. Margaret Schofield	—	Ticket to Heaven
16	By the Seaside	—	Ladies and Gentlemen of the Chorus
17	Down at the Old Bull and Bush	—	Full Company, but mainly Yourselves

The Bar will be open during the interval and after the performance.

1983

Breach of Promise was written for the society as a prelude to **Trial by Jury** and both were performed during March. Trial was the second half answer to Breach of Promise. The show included such songs as "I'd do anything", "Where is love" and "Oom-pah-pah".

October saw another G and S, this time **The Sorcerer** produced by Vivienne Aitken, her first with the society in this role.

1983 : The Sorcerer

Anthony Nixon as Alexis and Pamela Lander as Aline

Jean Oldaker as Constance and Bernard Vick as the Notary

1984

Two American visitors were in the audience at an early performance of **HMS Pinafore** and were so intrigued and excited at seeing amateurs act and sing, they booked tickets for other nights and appeared with their cameras. Apparently, according to our American friends, amateurs either act or sing in their country, but not both together. However, the society benefited from a large number of photographs supplied from the USA and kept in our archives. *(see colour plates for two fine colour pictures of cast members)*

During December CAOS staged an **Old Tyme Music Hall** which raised a profit of £573 which was donated to St Wilfrid's Hospice.

1985

To commemorate the society's 75th birthday, CAOS was presented with its own badge by the then mayor of the city, Mr Colin Tupper. Made possible by a legacy of £100 from former vice-president Mr Harry Ludlow, the badge was made by Mr Peter Cam, a master carpenter from Oving, and designed and painted by Mrs Pamela Vaughan, both being acting members of the society. The badge was proudly displayed at all performances for many years.

On Gala Day in Chichester, a float was entered in the parade depicting many Gilbert and Sullivan operas which CAOS had staged during its 75 years. First prize was presented to CAOS as winners of the general section.

Yeomen of the Guard was the chosen G and S for the year and was held at the Assembly Room during June. This was to be the last time that G and S was automatically chosen and plans were laid to widen the society's repertoire and consider more in the way of popular musicals.

Scrooge was chosen for December in the lead up to Christmas and proved to be a popular choice. It certainly made Christmas special for one dear lady who commented "it showed me the true meaning for this time of year and made me enjoy Christmas so much."

1985 : above: Scrooge! Previous page below: Tim Russell as the boy Scrooge and Polly Meynell as Sister Fan

1986

True to commitment, the committee chose a grand musical for 1986, Franz Lehar's **The Merry Widow**. It was a great success, reported in the press as follows: "Anyone fearing this step into the unknown might be like walking down a blind alley and that the competent group should stick to what they know best has no cause for worry, as the society is proving it can conjure up magic with whatever it handles." The report continues: "The The Merry Widow could not have been merrier and showed clearly that at the very least the society is capable and competent as well as versatile and talented." *(see colour section for two cast photographs.)*

Patience staged in November was mentioned as a "not only a virtue but also a hit." *(see photos opposite)*

1987

G and S was chosen for June with the very popular **Mikado**. This time it was reported "fine vocals and lavish costumes, with a lesson or two for the professionals."

1986 : Patience

Brian Oldaker as Grosvenor with chorus of maidens

"Soldiers of the Queen"

Musical Director Michael Walsh after receiving a gift of a fine silhouette of himself at the aftershow party

1987 : The Mikado

above: Philip Storer with Vivienne Aitken in full flight as Katisha

This was followed in December by a drama to music **While Shepherds Watched**. Performances were given at St Andrew's Church Oving, Christ Church and St George's Whyke, Chichester.

1988

CAOS year commenced with a concert on 12th March in aid of the mayor of Chichester's charity, Chichester and district Age Concern. The selections were chosen from The Pirates of Penzance, The Mikado, The Merry Widow and Waltzes from Vienna.

Waltzes from Vienna was staged at the Assembly Room during July and although praises for the production, costumes and performances were high, audiences did not come up to expectations. **A Music Hall** followed in November when, quite appropriately for Armistice Day, a scene of the First World War songs was produced. It was suggested that whilst *Keep the Home Fires Burning* was being sung, poppies should be scattered from above the stage. This was arranged and tears were shed in the audience, with one daughter asking her mother if she could borrow her handkerchief and receiving the reply, "Sorry, I'm using it."

1988 : Waltzes from Vienna Geoff Miller (Strauss the Elder), Simon Long (Strauss the Younger) and Ron Williams (Drexler)

1988: Delights of Music Hall ~ Tyrolean Melody

1988: Delights of Music Hall ~ "Good Old Summertime"

1989

A return to Gilbert and Sullivan with **The Gondoliers** at the Assembly Room during June. Bernard Vick, an enthusiastic and the long-serving member of CAOS, was presented with a life membership to mark a musical 50 years with the company.

1989: The Gondoliers ~ photo call

1989 : The Merry Widow ~ Geoff Porter as Danilo

During July, the Society arranged a concert during the Chichester Festivities billed as **Some Enchanted Evening** and raised £450 for the Observer Scanner Appeal.

At last the Society had room to stage a musical without cramping its performers. The first production at the Minerva Theatre was quite an experience for the chorus; no longer any back row to hide in, everyone could be seen. Because of past experience and its great popularity, **The Merry Widow** was chosen and again proved to be a great success. Audiences were near to capacity and exceeded all expectations.

1990

Trial by Jury and **Pirates of Penzance** at the Assembly Room was followed by **Carousel** at the Minerva Theatre. Many children were auditioned to take part in Carousel from as far afield as Lee on Solent and Bognor Regis. Two groups of nine children took part in the show and apparently enjoyed every moment, as did the audience.

1990 : Pirates of Penzance ~ "When the foeman bares his steel"
Jeff Miller, Jeff Stanbridge, John Davidson & Roger Ness

1990 : Pirates of Penzance ~ Kenton Budd as the Pirate King

1990 : Carousel ~ Kerry Joyce and Tony Bryant

1991 : Carousel ~ Ray Bill, Simon Long and Julie Matthews

1991

Brigadoon during the 80th year caused a few staging problems at the Assembly Room, but these were overcome and resulted in a very enjoyable show.

1991 : Brigadoon ~ Jane Newell 'Waitin' for my dearie'

1991 : Brigadoon ~ Mike Ofield, Geoff Miller and Jane Newell

It was decided that Gilbert and Sullivan's **Yeomen of the Guard** would be the ideal opera for the Minerva. The Arena proved wonderful to stage scenes where Yeomen and villagers mixed with room to move.

1992

Although not the most popular of operas, **Princess Ida** proved a great success with a great deal of comedy injected by producer Audrey Pring. During July, the Society presented **CAOS in Europe**, the musical tour of Europe, at St Paul's Church, Northgate. This included such songs as Tulips from Amsterdam, Neapolitan Medley, Frère Jacques, Danny Boy and many more.

To complete another successful year – **Oklahoma** at the Minerva Theatre. According to the press report, "among the most enjoyable shows Chichester Amateur Operatic Society has staged in years." Certainly the cast thoroughly enjoyed it.

1992 : Princess Ida ~ Simon Long (Cyril), Ian Somerville (Florian) and David Bathurst (Hilarion)

1992 : Oklahoma! ~ Mary-Rose Austin as Ado Annie

1993

Back to **The Delights of Music Hall** during February with scenes ranging from London to Broadway.

This was followed in May by **H.M.S. Pinafore**, successful despite a limited budget and a rather depleted membership. Sea shanties preceded the show, giving the chorus a chance to take the spotlight.

Illness threatened to ruin the CAOS production of **The Mikado** at the Minerva Theatre in November. Leading lady Alison Mobbs and one of the principal players Lizzie Bathurst were silenced by laryngitis and had to walk their parts. Kym Wilcocks of Havant Light Opera sang the part of Yum-Yum from the wings at less than four hours' notice, while Jean Oldaker came from the chorus to sing an engaging Peep-Bo.

1994

A touch of magic pervaded the Assembly room during June when CAOS presented **The Sorcerer.**

Die Fledermaus was staged at the Minerva during November, summed up by the press as: "ravishing razzle – dazzle to relish." *(see photo in colour section)*

An interesting statement appeared in the Observer which should be noted for the future: – "Amateur access was always central to Lesley Evershed Martin's theatrical vision for Chichester Festival Theatre. So how fitting it was to see Chichester Amateur Operatic Society in Minerva residence for its most ambitious production Die Fledermaus."

1995

Variety, pantomime, comedy and pathos were all contained in **Underneath the Arches** performed in May. Broken Blossoms performed by the CAOS crazy gang dressed as flower girls caused quite a riot, as did the show of their legs in the pantomime sequence.

1993 : Delights of Music Hall

'Sweet and Low' conducted by Vivienne Aitken

1993 : Delights of Music Hall ~ Barry Tester 'On the Range'

1994 : The Sorcerer ~

(left) Chris Shanks as Dr Daly

(below) Sarah Jerling as Constance and Barbara Stevens as Mrs Partlet

1994 : Die Fledermaus ~ The Warders

1994 : Die Fledermaus ~

Robert Brittain as Dr Falke (The Bat)

1995 : Underneath the Arches ~

right ~

Peter Hall as Chesney Allen and Ray Treagust as Bud Flanagan

below ~

The Crazy Gang 'Pantomime'

Kismet followed at the Minerva, being a complete contrast to the previous show with all the colour and romance of an Arabian night. A magical trip to Persia which held the audience spellbound – the press tell us – and who would argue? *(see colour photograph section)*

The busy year ended on the 15th December with a **Concert for the St Wilfrid's Hospice** conducted by Vivienne Aitken. Christmas music and carols were sung during the first half of the programme followed by **Night of Miracles** by John W Peterson.

1996

Costumes and colour certainly helped to make a show enjoyable and interesting and **The Gondoliers** had both of these in abundance together with a very strong principal cast.

1996 : The Gondoliers

Sarah Jerling as The Duchess of Plaza-Toro and Connie Archer as Inez

1996 : Fiddler on the Roof

above: Christopher Doman as Tevye and Margaret Leach as Golde

below: members of the chorus

Not exactly a cheery story, but nevertheless a great success, was **Fiddler on the Roof** at the Minerva Theatre during October. The show, which ran for more than two and a half hours, produced a convincing atmosphere of Russian village life.

Light entertainment again with another **Delights of Music Hall**, giving newcomers to the Society a chance to shine. One adverse criticism was heard, in the Dutch scene, apparently the windmill was turning the wrong way!

1996 : More Delights of Music Hall

right:
Margaret Leach

'When I take my morning promenade"

below:
'Springtime in Holland'

Some of the stars - Kym Willcocks, Lizzie Bathhurst, Kay Newell, Jean Oldaker.

'Pirates' getting ready

Rehearsals – and tickets – are going well for for the next production from Chichester Amateur Operatic Society.

Madeline Doman is producing The Pirates Of Penzance for CAOS at Chichester's Minerva Theatre from November 4 to 8.

Among her stars are Kym Willcocks, Lizzie Bathurst, Kay Newell and Jean Oldaker.

Kym has previously played leads in The Gondoliers, Kismet and Die Fledermaus. Lizzie has been seen in HMS Pinafore. Jean was in Fiddler On The Roof last year.

Tickets are available from the Festival Theatre.

Pirates of Penzance was staged at the Minerva during November under producer Madeline Doman and musical director Arthur Robson.

1998

CAOS obtained the services of the much–in-demand Doreen Wilde to produce **Waltzes from Vienna** during June at the Assembly Room. Doreen produces three or four productions a year and says "I am a widow, and it's a rather nice hobby." Certainly she produced a super show for CAOS, enjoyed by audience and cast alike.

A sparkling and enjoyable production of Lerner and Lowe's legendary musical **My Fair Lady** followed during December at the Minerva. Directed by Sally Davis, a former Tiller Girl, with musical director Michael Walsh, the show was originally planned for November. The Minerva, however, extended the period for a successful professional show and CAOS was rescheduled for December. *(see colour photos)*

1998 : Waltzes from Vienna ~ 'Is it worth it?'
l to r: John Mason, Alan Thresher, Peter Hall, Ray Treagust

1998 : My Fair Lady ~ David Bennett as Colonel Pickering

1998 : My Fair Lady ~ Peter Fray as Henry Higgins, Brian Mattack as Alfred Doolittle and Audrey Rogers as Mrs. Pearce

1999

Vivienne Clark produced **HMS Pinafore** during May. Problems were experienced with the leading role of Ralph Rackstraw, but CAOS were able, with only a few rehearsals to go, to obtain the excellent acting experience of Ian Clark from Selsey Operatic Society. **Half a Sixpence** was staged at the Minerva in November and although it was a super show, did not attract the audience it deserved.

2000

And so to 90 years of CAOS; quite a year it was too. Kathryn Wignall produced a stunning **Oklahoma** at the Assembly Room in May, full of action and movement. The scenery, so simple and yet so effective, was the subject of admiration by many, and was designed as usual by Roger Ness. (What would CAOS have done without him?)

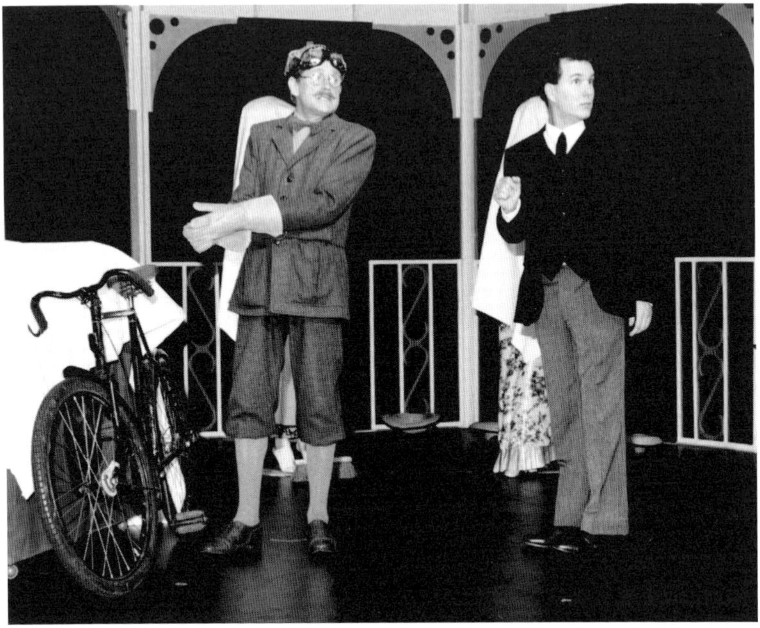

1999 : Half a Sixpence
above: Kevin Cassidy as Chitterlow and Ian Clark as Kipps

below: Ann Bray and Georgina Godfrey

2000 : Oklahoma!

right:
Simon Long as Curly and
David Russell as Jud Fry

below:

Nicola Russell
as Ado Annie and
John Warner
as Will Parker

On 14th July, **90 Years of CAOS**, a concert, was presented at St John's Church. The first half of the concert was mainly Gilbert and Sullivan, followed by a second half of musical items from a variety of other shows performed by the Society.

Scrooge took the stage in November and although rehearsal time was short, combined with Trial by Jury, it proved another successful production. CAOS's 90th year was certainly a busy one, finishing on 8th December with a Christmas concert and on the following day a Christmas Fayre. Rather than the normal carol concert it was decided to include mainly Christmas music with just a few carols for the audience to join in with. This proved to be a successful combination and was enjoyed by all.

2000 : Scrooge
l to r: Nicola Russell, Sue Marchant, Margaret Leach, Paul Green and Luke Hopkins as Tiny Tim

above : 2000 : Scrooge ~ Liz McNally as Polly and Ray Treagust as Scrooge

below : 2001 : Yeomen of the Guard
(left) Veronica Kirby as Elsie Maynard and (right) Helen Claxton-Roper as Phoebe

2002

Finding a venue for the Society became even more difficult and we were both delighted and relieved to be given the chance to perform at the Roman Palace at Fishbourne. The question being, what can or rather what would be appropriate to enact, given the location. John Mason had the wonderful idea of adapting from a Gilbert and Sullivan operetta, **Iolanthe in Rome or The Senator and the Virgin**. It proved a great success and the Society were able to donate a substantial sum to the Roman Palace.

During November it was arranged that we should have a **Victorian evening**, inviting people to entertainment with music from the Victorian era together with supper. Originally this was arranged to be performed at the Assembly Room, however, due to very poor acoustics, Victorian Songbook was switched to St Wilfrid's Church Hall at the last moment. It proved to be a delightful evening, and as one lady wrote to the Observer, "The roof of the hall nearly blew off twice to happy singing."

2002 : Iolanthe in Rome ~ (left) Vivienne and Robert Clark, (right) Douglas Meadway and David Russell

2003

Still without a permanent venue we again performed at the Roman Palace with **The Pirates of Penzance**. It was noted a skeleton lay on the floor in the Palace but we were assured it was not one of last year's audience. Although the performance itself went quite well, it was considered both the stage and scenery were quite inadequate.

2003 : Pirates of Penzance ~
Simon Long as Frederic and Rebecca Grove as Mabel

At last the Society's prayers and hard work were rewarded; we were back at the Minerva during October with **Annie Get Your Gun**. With an American musical and a professional venue, we attracted a number of new younger members, the lifeblood of any society. With new members, also a new audience and a real boost for CAOS. The show could only be a great success.

To bring the year to a grand finale, a **Christmas concert** including John Peterson's *The Wonder of Christmas* was staged at St Wilfrid's Church Hall during December, together with traditional mulled wine and mince pies. 2003 proved a shot in the arm for the Society. It was during 2003 that the Society changed its name to CAOS Musical Productions to

2003: Annie Get Your Gun

Stephanie Treagust as Annie Oakley and Jason Walby as Frank Butler

Below:

the cast

reflect the new style of performances undertaken by the Society.

Also that year, three members of CAOS received the coveted gold bar from the National Operatic and Dramatic Association. The NODA medals acknowledged 50 years of unbroken service from John Mason, Ann Bray and Keith Parker.

Sadness also struck the Society with the loss of Phyllis Pointing in March 2003, followed by Marjorie Mollie de Pennington and Bernard Victor Vick in 2004. All three were long serving and dedicated members of the Society.

2004

"Ingenious ideas and an enthralling production" appeared in NODA Southern News relating to the October performance of **Carousel** at the Minerva Theatre. Several years previously the Society made a hefty loss at the Minerva but in spite of high costs we crept into the black with Carousel. Amateurs were giving professional quality performances in the professional theatre.

2004 : Carousel ~ The Graduation scene

2004 : Carousel ~ Kenton Budd as Billy Bigelow

Another first for the Society was a performance with the Chichester Symphony Orchestra of **Hiawatha's Wedding Feast** and **Captain Noah and His Floating Zoo**. The performance took place in St Paul's Church under the direction of Michael Walsh.

2005

CAOS paid tribute to those who served in World War II in a show created to mark the 60th anniversary of the end of hostilities. Vera Lynn was invited to introduce the show **Let the People Sing**, but unfortunately she had a previous engagement. However, she kindly recorded a message which was played to the audience before each performance. The music included many wartime favourites such as

2005 : 'Let the People Sing'

Quartermasters' Stores, When The Lights Go on Again, The White Cliffs of Dover and many, many more.

The **Mikado** followed in October at the Minerva and with an excellent cast, proved to be a great success, both artistically and financially. Vivienne Clark took the part of Katisha but sadly, due to illness, this was to be Vivienne's last performance with CAOS.

2006

Commenced with a concert version of **Merrie England**, music by Edward German. During the performance on the 80th birthday of the Queen, the Mayor of Chichester led everyone in a rousing chorus of "Happy Birthday, Your Majesty."

CAOS performed Sandy Wilson's popular musical, **The Boyfriend** during November, attracting a number of new, talented young people to the Society. The ingenious

2005 : The Mikado

above: John Warner as the Mikado and Vivienne Clark as Katisha

right:

Nicola Russell as Yum Yum and Jason Walby as Nanki-Poo

2006 : The Boyfriend ~
above: John Butt and Meg Saulet as Lord and Lady Brockhurst

below: The Company

2006: The Boyfriend

Downstairs at the Minerva:

Above: Tracey Stone, Helen Claxton-Roper and Sue Marchant as three maids

Left: fashionable ladies

Christine McCarthy, Elizabeth Peacock, Val Creswick, Sue Marchant and Rebecca Grove

2006: The Boyfriend

John 'Chalky' White with Elizabeth Peacock

2006: The Boyfriend

Clockwise from top left: Charlie Tarrant, Matthew Hughes-Short, Jason Walby, Danny Coltan

set designed by Roger Ness, colourful costumes and a wonderfully energetic cast, directed meticulously by Kathryn Wignall, ensured an outstanding success.

Vivienne Clark, a life member of the Society, passed away at the age of 60 on December 28th. She had served CAOS as Musical Director, Producer, Soloist and Seamstress.

2007

Another demanding concert **From the Pirate to the Phantom** put CAOS through their paces in a wide-ranging musical entertainment. The show commenced with G and S followed by a selection from *Les Miserables.* Five medleys were included in the second half from *Oklahoma, The King and I, South Pacific, My Fair Lady* and a final selection of music by Andrew Lloyd Webber.

2007 : 'From the Pirate to the Phantom'

Brigadoon won the Society an "accolade of excellence" from NODA. The NODA representative Roy Brown admitted that Brigadoon was not one of his favourite shows, but he highly commended the production being sparkling, full of life with many fine individual performances. Congratulations were forthcoming to Director Patricia Roberts, Musical Director Michael Walsh and Wardrobe Mistress Elizabeth Peacock.

2007: Brigadoon ~ Catherine O'Hanlon and Stephen O'Shea

2008

Viennese music greeted our Chichester audience during May with such lovely melodies as *Danube, River of Dreams* and *The Merry Widow Waltz.* **A Viennese Gala** was provided with a chorus of over thirty voices.

Die Fledermaus was performed in the Minerva Theatre at the end of October. People who saw the show commented on its excellence, but unfortunately it did not attract the audience expected. It is thought the title of the show possibly gave people the impression that it was indeed opera. During the year, charity performances were given at Lordington Park residential and convalescent home, Covers for their Children's Christmas treat and St Anne's Church, East Wittering for their Christmas Tree Festival. We believe this not only gave people enjoyment, but also provided a different sort of venue and added experience for younger society members.

2009 : Die Fledermaus ~ Matthew Hughes-Short as Prince Orlofsky

2009 : Die Fledermaus ~

above: Margo Dodd as Ida and and Robert Clark as Doctor Falke

below: Amanda Crehan as Rosalinda and David Russell as Gabriel Eisenstein

2009

"Here's a bit of CAOS you'd be mad to avoid," or so wrote Phil Hewitt in The Chichester Observer. He was of course referring to **Guys and Dolls** with its choreographed big numbers mixed with solos, duets and a great chorus.

Again, new talent appeared in the shape of young performers. The show was directed by Kathryn Wignall with Musical Director, Paula McGovern. This time the cast were delighted to play to full houses. (*see colour section for more photos*)

Comparison – it cost just a few pounds to put on a show during the early years of CAOS. Present day costs for productions at the Minerva Theatre are between £20,000 – £30,000.

Where will it end?

2009 : Guys and Dolls

Peter Roper as Big Jule

Jim Strudwick with Catherine O'Hanlon

2009: Guys and Dolls

Kerrie Wenham as Sgt. Sarah Brown

2010

Hello, Dolly! completed our century in spectacular style, with a cast of 43 performers including a wonderful male chorus which would be the envy of many amateur societies. The show nearly didn't happen when we had difficulty recruiting young men for the team of dancing waiters, but the eventual team of ten were a triumph.

2010: Hello, Dolly!

Ashley Tickell as Minnie Fay

Unusually, the weather caused quite a problem during the rehearsals for the show, with some having to be cancelled and rescheduled due to the snow and people being unable to attend. However, the show was beautifully directed and choreographed by Kathryn Wignall. The musical was superbly dressed using 160 costumes, many of them made and supplied by CAOS's hard-working chairman Elizabeth Peacock and assisted by Georgina Godfrey, who also masterminded all the props needed for this production.

The main role of Dolly was played by Amanda Crehan, ably supported by Kevin Cassidy as Horace Vandergelder. All of the main characters had been well cast and gave their all, resulting in a highly successful finale.

There was a near-disaster on the second night of the show when Amanda was struck down with illness and her understudy, Christine Henry, had to stand in at very short notice. Christine did a magnificent job; likewise Jason Walby had to be put on standby as Trevor Thurgood reported similar symptoms as well, but in the end Trevor took to the stage and gave his usual fine performance. CAOS's decision to have understudies properly prepared was certainly vindicated that night!

Final mention must be made of the musical direction in the capable hands of Paula McGovern.

2010 Hello, Dolly!

Two of the dancing waiters: Peter Hall and Romaric Masson.

(see colour section for more photos)

A COMEDY OF ERRORS
(or chaos reigns)

During any show, professional or amateur, things do (just occasionally) go wrong, sometimes very wrong, however well organised, but the show must go on. Over 100 years, CAOS is no exception and listed below are just some of those occasions, intentional and unintentional.

The late Len Marchant once recalled being in the Mikado, standing to attention with the men's chorus and holding a wooden stave at the slope with his right hand. He explained that all the girls, wearing the traditional black wigs, were sitting and kneeling on the stage. Len apparently felt a tug on his costume and saw a girl (he called her a bald headed eagle) pointing to his stave, on which hung her wig.

Keith Parker also experienced a problem in this opera whilst playing the role of the Mikado. One evening, when just going into the Mikado's song, he flipped open his rather large fan with accustomed vigour and heard an unaccustomed cracking noise from his right. Obviously, he had hit something but could not stop to look, due to the musical introduction and entry into his song. However, it transpired that he had hit Carol Nighy, standing in the chorus-line, a nice hard blow straight on top of the head. How to win friends!

Bernard Vick recalled that during his first show with the Society, Pirates of Penzance in 1938 at the Corn Exchange, chaos really did reign. Apparently it was during the policeman's chorus. The backcloth, held up by four inch by two inch timber, collapsed onto the stage, leaving the chorus struggling underneath. It was necessary to close the main curtain to enable the cast to free themselves and carry off a stunned Reginald Bevis, who appears to have been saved from serious injury because he was wearing a policeman's helmet. One way of bringing the house down!

During the sentry's song in a performance of Iolanthe it was decided that a stork should fly overhead. John Glover duly rigged one on a wire and it worked perfectly. One night however, someone (who shall remain nameless) released the stork on cue, but unfortunately when the bird reached the other side of the stage, the wire should have been pulled tight to secure it in position. The wire was left slack resulting, to used John's words:- "One stork slid backwards into the middle of the stage, he coughed and sailed off again."

Wooden crates have often been used to raise backstage, causing quite a number of problems. During the 1973 production of The Sorcerer, orange boxes were laid end to end across the stage and covered in baize. At the beginning of Act 2 the chorus lay asleep on the stage, affected by the love potion administered by John Wellington Wells. Three main characters, Aline (Paddy Dornom), Alexis (Keith Parker) and John Wellington Wells (John Mason) were singing the opening trio. Whilst Wells was performing his solo part, Aline and Alexis were to turn outwards, take six steps along the orange box plinth, stop, turn inwards and walk back in. Those were the instructions. On Thursday night, Keith unfortunately did not manage the six steps required as stage management had not laid out the correct number of boxes. During this very quiet scene he fell flat on his face with a great thud accompanied by the clatter of his sword scabbard. How can you expect the chorus to sleep?

The same week in the finale of Act 1, Paddy entered in her wedding dress and walked towards the notary (Bernard Vick) for the signing of the register. However, on entering the stage, Paddy's dress caught on a piece of protruding metal from an orange box and this box was towed behind her, down to the front of the stage. It is understood that audience and cast were in hysterics; this did not, however, include the producer.

During a production of The Gondoliers an entirely different problem was experienced. The beautiful gondola entered at the scene, perfectly polled by a gondolier. After delivering his two passengers, the gondolier posed with his pole to exit left but unfortunately the craft had been rigged to exit right, result: one rather foolish looking gondolier punting offstage backwards.

Back to crates once again being used to raise the stage. During Iolanthe, the Peers made their stately entry along a row of upturned, covered crates. It was noticed that one crate midstage had split. What the audience would have enjoyed was to have seen the backstage crew standing in the wings holding a chalked message over their heads "Mind the 4th one!" – and praying hard.

Bernard Vick also relates a little problem he had during a Carol Concert at the Assembly Room. The Society were standing in front of the stage, accompanied in their singing by the Chichester City Band, who were accommodated on the stage. Whilst lustily singing 'O come all ye faithful', Bernard's new dentures (which incidentally he had only had for three days and were quite expensive) flew out of his mouth. Chichester's Mayor, who was sitting in the front row, received the teeth on his shoulder, but unfortunately they didn't stay there. They slid down the mayor's arm and disappeared from view. Bernard became rather concerned, partly because of the cost of the teeth and spent some time on his hands and knees, feeling between the Mayoress's feet where he was eventually successful. It appears the Mayor enjoyed the episode, saying: "It's the funniest thing that has happened since we took office." Moral – don't sing falsetto.

Many laughs have occurred in the dressing rooms. One amusing incident occurred relating to food. It was quite normal between the matinee and Saturday evening performance to have a communal meal of fish and chips. On this particular occasion the list requesting names of people ordering their meal was hung in the dressing room as usual. First name on the list was Alf Price, consequently the list actually read 'fish and chips Alf price.'

For a great number of years the final performance of any show was also a time for practical jokes, a habit which we are pleased to have stopped. On one occasion during Patience, John Glover handed each lady a harp as they ran on stage, all that is except the last lady, Molly de Pennington, who found herself in charge of a toilet seat.

* * * * *

As previously mentioned, the success of CAOS would not have been possible without the dedication and hard work of a great number of people. However, it would not be correct to mention any particular names as it is inevitable that a number of people would, unfortunately, be omitted.

For those of you who have, and do, support the Society, either by helping backstage, front of house or as a member of the audience, you deserve to have the grateful thanks of every CAOS member.

Ray Treagust

December 2009